"I dream of an Africa which is in peace with itself" | *Nelson Mandela*

SOUTH AFRICA

a journey in pictures | SOUTH AFRICA

South Africa – a vast sub-continent of rugged mountains and rich farmland; golden beaches and great natural wonders. From a priceless wildlife heritage and the elusive Big Five that roam the sundrenched savannah, to a magnificent array of indigenous wild flowers and graceful birdlife, South Africa is a glittering showcase of nature's most colourful creations. From shore to golden shore, across the great plains and deep canyons, mighty mountains and gentle valleys - a geographic masterpiece of immense proportions, spread beneath a big African sky. This nation echoes with stories of battles won and lost; a land renowned for its turbulent history and vibrant people; a nation applauded by the world community as a young democracy, boldly forging new frontiers and building a brighter future. Welcome to a photographic journey across this rainbow nation of sunshine, splendour and unsurpassed scenic beauty – a world in one country.

| *Table Mountain from Bloubergstrand*

Robben Island lies eleven kilometres off the Peninsula mainland, a small island destined to be forever synonymous with South Africa's struggle for freedom. Robben Island remains infamous for its maximum security prison which, for 27 years, incarcerated Nelson Mandela, charismatic past President of the fledgling democracy, and others who have dedicated their very existence to guiding the nation toward a greater future.

"There is nothing like returning to a place that remains unchanged to find the ways in which you yourself have altered" | *Nelson Mandela*

A friendly disposition, spectacular beaches, rocky coastline and mountainous profile have earned the Cape a reputation as "The Fairest Cape". Add to that a vibrant waterfront, an intriguing history, fine wines and superior cuisine at any of the superbly appointed restaurants across the Peninsula, and the result is a sunny tourist mecca that welcomes countless visitors from across the globe.

The flat-topped mass of Table Mountain is a familiar Cape landmark, and below it sprawls the pulsating city bowl, where the remnants of an early Dutch settlement stand proudly alongside modern structures, creating a city of charm and character. From extravagant mansions on the mountain slopes to the quaint and colourful homes of Cape Town's Malay Quarter, the city exudes a convivial and inviting atmosphere, steeped in culture and alive with the friendly demeanour of its people.

Through swirling sea mists, Cape Town glitters at the foot of the familiar landmark that has beckoned seafarers through the ages | 13

As twilight cloaks the city with a golden hue, the cable car rotates leisurely, ferrying visitors to the summit of Table Mountain for a breathtaking ride

18 | *The conical Lion's Head amidst the clouds* | *The unique style and colourful disposition of the Malay Quarter, Bo-Kaap*

Exclusive Clifton beach meets the ocean at the foot of the mighty Twelve Apostles, the cliffs at the western edge of Table Mountain

The popular resort town of Hout Bay along the scenic Chapman's Peak Drive | 21

·Cape Point, a jagged rocky headland pounded relentlessly by a turbulent Atlantic Ocean | 23

At Cape Point, the southernmost tip of the Cape Peninsula, the great continent of Africa tumbles from precipitous heights into a cold Atlantic, and waves rise from mysterious depths to vent their fury on this isolated headland. The roar of the sea as it smashes against a rocky shoreline leaves a lasting impression on those who have stood at land's end, looking out to sea. Little wonder that this rugged coast, so mercilessly exploited by the elements, is a haven of age-old rock, pitted and sculpted to curious shapes. Cape Point is part of the Cape of Good Hope Nature Reserve, a world of unlimited fascination where bontebok and eland roam and Cape cormorants circle above indigenous fynbos species. It is also one of the richest floral kingdoms in the world. This place of unsurpassed, unspoilt loveliness is unquestionably Nature's realm, where man is welcome to take only memories, and leave only footprints..

Boulders Beach near Simonstown, home to a breeding colony of African penguins

The quaint harbour of Kalk Bay along the east coast of the Peninsula | 29

Rows of lush green vines, nurtured to yield a substantial harvest, at an estate along the Paarl Wine Route

Cape Winelands | SOUTH AFRICA

A glass of fruity white wine on a Cape summer's day, or a hearty rich red at the fireside in winter: fine wines are an integral part of the Cape experience. Whitewashed gabled Cape Dutch homesteads, nestling amidst the vines, recall the early days of winemaking, while today's winemasters bring technological skills to a vibrant industry, the pride of the Cape. From the vines of Groot Constantia – the Cape's oldest vineyard, established by the early Dutch settlers in the late 1600s – to the vast estates in Paarl, Stellenbosch and beyond, the Cape is wine country, and connoisseurs the world over acknowledge the quality and finesse of a Cape wine. The wine estates have also become renowned for inspiring the delicate art of haute cuisine, and world-class restaurants and guesthouses proliferate along each route.

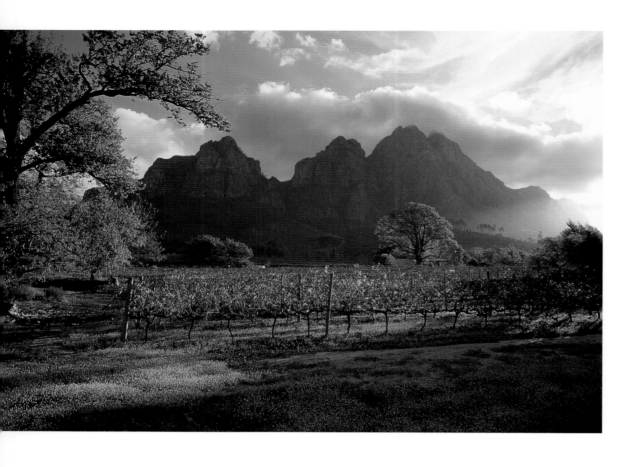

Autumn vines bring a fiery glow to a mountain backdrop at Simonsberg near Franschhoek | *Snow-capped peaks at Worcester*

Brilliant sunshine-yellow fields of canola stretch to the horizon in the Overberg

The Overberg & Southern Cape | SOUTH AFRICA

Brilliant sunshine-yellow fields of canola alternate with healthy wheatfields, weaving a colourful patchwork across the undulating rural landscape of the Overberg. At the town of Caledon, springs of clear mountain water bubble to the surface; picturesque country villages like Greyton preserve the flavour of life in the Cape in an age gone by, neatly spread across valleys of fertile farmland in the shadow of graceful mountain ridges.

Windswept dunes at De Hoop Nature Reserve on the Cape's southern coastline

Cape Agulhas, a scattering of cottages and a consistent beam of light from the world's most southerly lighthouse salute the great continent of Africa as it slips beneath the breakers of the Indian Ocean. Memories of sunken ships from days gone by resound at Cape Agulhas, Africa's southernmost point. Miles of unspoilt coast blessed with rich marine life add to the allure of this remote coastal treasure.

The Cape West Coast | SOUTH AFRICA

The western coastline of the Cape is washed by the Benguela current, which brings great shoals of pilchards and anchovies – and subsequently, a flourishing fishing industry. The magnificent bay of Saldanha is South Africa's largest natural harbour.

Beyond the curve of picturesque St Helena Bay, the town of Velddrif is the centre of the 'bokkem' industry – a salty, savoury snack of fish, hung in rows to dry in the sea air. Whitewashed fishing cottages and cool white sands fringe a scenic bay at the nearby settlement of Paternoster.

A green belt of spectacular scenery, known appropriately as The Garden Route, stretches over 280km from Mossel Bay to distant Cape St Francis. Beyond is the Eastern Cape, which embraces friendly towns like East London and Port Elizabeth; and inland is the Little Karoo, a remote expanse of rich farmland dotted with historic towns and boasting some of the greatest mountain passes in the country.

The Garden Route is a natural treasure trove of forests and rocky inlets, resort towns and sun-soaked beaches strewn with shells and the footprints of holidaymakers. This magnificent coastline is an Eden of contrasting beauty. The endless dunes and wide, windswept beaches at Wilderness. The tiny enclave of Victoria Bay – a haven for surfers. Sunsets reflected on the lagoon near the artists' hamlet of Sedgefield. The tranquillity of Buffels Bay. A coastal rain forest of Yellowwood, Stinkwood and Ironwood trees at Tsitsikamma Forest National Park. The holiday atmosphere that prevails at Knysna, Plettenberg Bay and Keurbooms Lagoon. And the perilously steep gorges at Storms River.

This gem of the South African coastline is nature's garden, a paradise of unrivalled splendour.

Sunset over a typical Karoo landscape | 47

The Little Karoo lies between the Outeniqua and Great Swartberg ranges, a semi-dry region of endless farmlands stretching between the mountains, where even the meagre rainfall is greatly treasured.

Oudtshoorn nestles in this belt, a town where the curious ostrich - the largest flightless bird - watches life go by. The 23km long Swartberg Pass joins the Karoo town of Prince Albert with Oudtshoorn. En route, the zig-zag roadway traverses the Swartberg mountains that conceal the Cango Caves, one of the great wonders of the world. Limestone formations are caused by the dripping of mineral-rich water into caverns eroded by underground water through hundreds of thousands of years. This is a magical world of sculptured columns of bizarre proportions, some small and dainty, others large and hauntingly grotesque, concealed deep within the earth.

A road less travelled in this arid Little Karoo country

The Outeniqua Choo-Tjoe, one of the few remaining operational steam engines, offers a journey through breathtaking vistas between Knysna and George | 53

The town of Knysna is built on the banks of a vast lagoon, sprinkled with small islands and dotted with leisurecraft and ferries. The seaward entrance to the lagoon is guarded by two colossal sandstone cliffs, The Heads, which overlook a spectacular playground embued with a distinct holiday atmosphere.

A few kilometres east, Plettenberg Bay sparkles on a shimmering coastline. Glorious beaches invite sunworshippers, and the town's intimate restaurants and fascinating shops welcome visitors throughout the four seasons. Just beyond the promontory where the Beacon Isle Hotel overlooks a remarkable seascape, Robberg Nature Reserve juts out into the sea, a haven where the call of the cormorant is just audible above the crashing of the waves. The tranquil lagoons at Keurbooms, centuries-old trees at Tsitsikamma Forest, and the rugged rocky estuary at Storms River, all priceless heritage on this Garden Route of Africa.

Storms River enters the sea in dramatic style, a narrow channel of water slicing through high cliffs and deep rocky gorges before it widens to meet the Indian Ocean at a tranquil place of loveliness. The Paul Sauer Bridge arches high above this majestic vista, with a look-out across the rocky abyss and green wilderness. The river cuts through the Tsitsikamma National Park, an area of coastal heritage prized for its ecological significance and ancient trees, where it is rumoured that the last of the coastal elephant live a reclusive existence.

Sunset and sunrise over the seaside town of Port Elizabeth | 61

Dawn of a new day, Valley of Desolation near Graaff-Reinet

The Wild Coast | SOUTH AFRICA

Rolling green hills and a treacherous coastline ramble between the Eastern Cape and KwaZulu-Natal - the former Transkei, home of the Xhosa people. The Indian Ocean along this shoreline obscures the rusted wrecks of several sunken ships which attest to the untamed fury of the seas of this Wild coast. And yet, with its wilderness of mangrove-strewn river estuaries, rocky beaches and tangled indigenous forest, it is also a place of tranquillity and loveliness. Enormous formations of eroded rock stand proudly against the breakers… waterfalls plummet from sheer cliffs directly into the sea. This coastline has earned its rightful reputation as the Wild Coast of southern Africa.

Golden beaches and undulating hills of sugar cane, leafy suburbs and lush Midland farmland, historic battlefields and the majestic Drakensberg. This is the province of KwaZulu-Natal, alive with a cross-cultural blend of people. The home of the Zulu – a proud people with a history of warrior kings and tribal custom. A tropical temperament, summer weather most of the year and a refreshing Indian Ocean lend KwaZulu-Natal a holiday atmosphere that ripples from the smiling beachfront crafters, with their beaded wares and skillfully woven mats and baskets, to the green hills beyond Durban and across the mountains.

A summer breeze plays through the masts of the yachts in the small craft harbour and carries a spicy fragrance from the aromatic mixtures at the downtown market; sea mist drifts lazily off the ocean breakers: Durban comes to life as colourful umbrellas open against the heat at beachfront cafes.

Resort towns along the eastern seaboard, from Margate and Southbroom on the South Coast to Umhlanga and Ballito in the North, echo the leisurely holiday ambience of the province's principal city.

Aerial view of Durban, across a bustling harbour, a quaint yacht mole, the Victoria Embankment, to the inviting ocean beyond | 67

The tide ebbs, exposing miles of crisp golden beach: the Durban city skyline at sunrise | A warm Indian Ocean makes Durban a surfers paradise |

uShaka marine world, a place where sharks drift eerily in their deep blue surrounds and dolphins and seals put on a sterling performance; where visitors can touch a starfish, snorkel over rocky reefs and brightly-coloured coral, relax in the sun or splash down in a crystal clear pool after a roller-coaster water ride. Durban's uShaka Marine World is a thrilling and informative entertainment park; an opportunity to explore the wonders of life beneath the Indian Ocean breakers. Strategically positioned windows allow a privileged insight into the silent world of the sea creatures.

The South African coast is blessed with a rich and varied marine life. Consistently each year, during the winter months between May and July, millions of silvery sardines (mackerel) travel northward from the cold southerly oceans, staying close to the shoreline as they make their way up the eastern coastline, as far north as KwaZulu-Natal. This is the annual Sardine Run: sardine shoals moving in great masses, often as much as fifteen kilometres in length, over three kilometres wide and up to forty metres deep. The Sardine Run elicits a rush of publicity and great interest as hundreds of predators arrive en masse to join the feeding frenzy. Schools of dolphins, whales, sharks and game fish — and even the sea birds — add to this spectacle of the deep, gorging themselves on easy pickings.

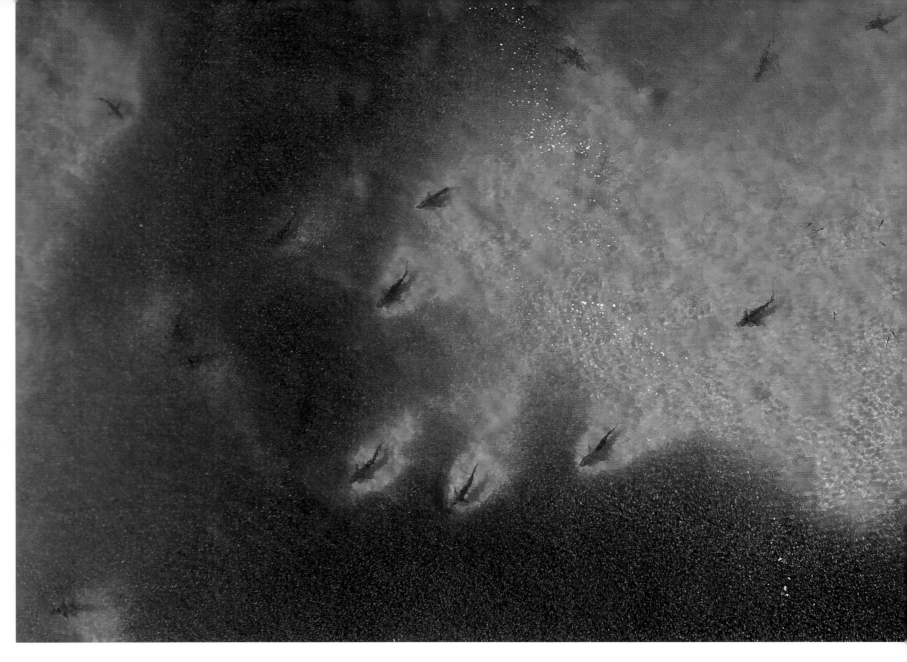

Along the KwaZulu-Natal South Coast, the water virtually boils with a mass of flickering silver bodies, providing an easy catch for sharks and fishermen alike | 73

Foamy breakers pound the rocky shoreline at the foot of the lighthouse at Umhlanga Rocks, North Coast | 75

Lake Sibiya, northern KwaZulu-Natal, a sanctuary for bird and marine life | 77

An Acacia tree silhouetted near the historic battlefield at Rorke's Drift | 81

The battlefields of KwaZulu-Natal, where the wind whistles through the wild grasses and weathered memorials stand as a reminder of those who fell in battle, time seems to stand still in reverence of those who fought on these battlefields. The redcoats of the British regiments… the resolute settler-farmers… the Zulu people, transformed from a clan into a mighty nation under the rule of warrior king Shaka. Historians marvel at how these people, armed with spears and shields and a handful of antiquated firearms, crushed the celebrated British troops at the battle of Isandlwana.

Sixty four bronze Voortrekker ox-wagons, in laager formation, mark the site of the Battle of Blood River | 83

Zulu youngsters splash in a cool river in rural KwaZulu-Natal | 85

Colourful cosmos on the banks of the uThukela River and the distant Amphitheatre

Drakensberg | SOUTH AFRICA

Beyond the foothills of the Midlands, the contours become increasingly steeper until at last the mighty Drakensberg mountains come into view. Craggy peaks reach to the heavens in a grand crescendo… green valleys echo with the sound of water cascading over the cliffs and into deep basins below, eroding great boulders as countless rivers journey to the sea. This is the place to nurture the soul; a place of wonder where silence pervades and the sheer height of the peaks inspires awe at every turn. High up on the plateau of this 'Barrier of Spears', several rivers have their source, creating spectacular gorges.

The Amphitheatre is a towering arc of crescent-shaped cliffs, a backdrop for some of the country's most inspiring scenery. The uKhahlamba Drakensberg Park has earned pride of place as a World Heritage Site – a place of particular environmental significance, recognised by the world community to be of outstanding universal value.

Jagged spires of rock interspersed with great basalt plateaux, well over 1000 metres above sea level, create an inspiring mountain backdrop

As the sun sets, silhouetting the mountai

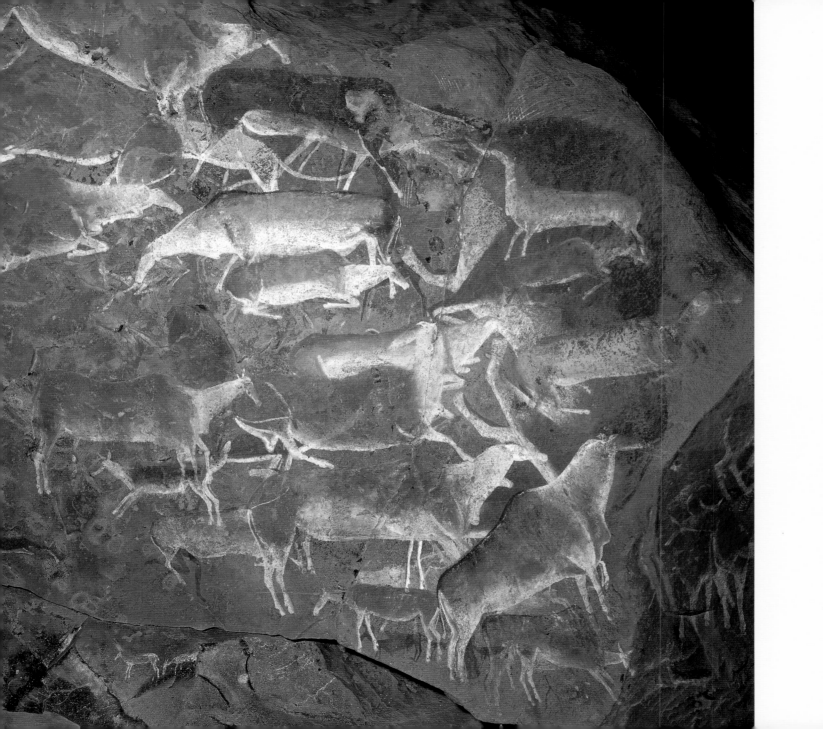

The majestic Drakensberg in particular, and much of the rest of southern Africa, is a showcase of priceless rock art, left as a legacy by the Bushman people. Rock paintings adorn many sandstone cave shelters, and provide vital clues to the culture, beliefs and inventiveness of a people who once thrived in the isolated valleys and foothills. The paintings depict hunting scenes, wild game, and tribal rituals such as the healing process taking place during a trance dance, with hallucinated visions brought to life on the rockface. Eland proliferate throughout the paintings, as the animal was regarded as having sacred links to their spiritual world.

The Drakensberg is a geographic feature of South Africa that extends from the Cape, forms a boundary with Lesotho at its highest points and continues through to Mpumalanga Province. Here, the cool allure of dense forests, misty country roads, plantations and waterfalls make for a dramatically beautiful rural landscape. Thousands of acres are devoted entirely to forestry, and several towns have grown up in the area specifically to serve the industry. Trout is on the menu in most parts, and hospitable country inns offer a welcome retreat for troutfishermen after a tranquil day's fishing. Rivers criss-cross Mpumalanga province, and create beautiful falls in cool grottos that beg to be explored. This is a mystical province of gold-mining towns and forest-clad roadways that echo with the memory of horse-drawn carriages from the days of the transport riders, and legends of settlers from far-off places who came in search of gold. Off-the-road lookouts reward today's travellers with views of craggy gorges, deep ravines and the green hills beyond.

Sunset reflected in one of Mpumalanga's many rivers | 97

Flame-coloured aloes frame the view from Graskop to God's Window

farmlands in rural Mpumalanga Province

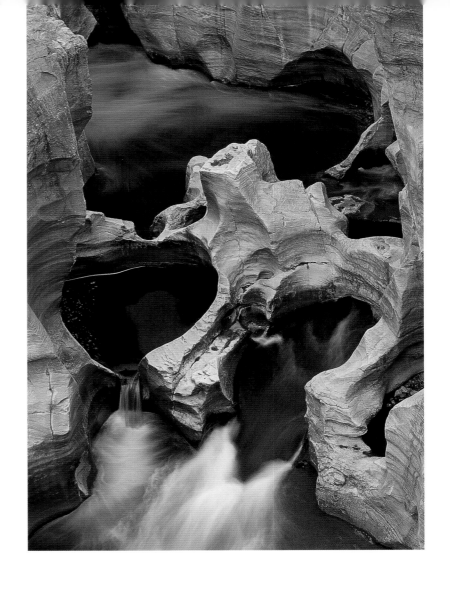

Water plummets into a rocky basin at Lone Creek falls near Sabie | *Water in motion creates curious rock formations at Bourke's Luck Potholes* |

Intriguing stories of the changing fortunes of gold prospectors add to the appeal of Mpumalanga province. The village of Pilgrim's Rest preserves the grandeur of the Victorian age, and buildings flaunt the patina of a bygone era – a memory of the gold-rush days. Gold was first discovered in these remote rural parts in 1873, and illicited a flurry of excitement with prospectors arriving in search of fame and fortune. Today, Mpumalanga remains a lush green corner of the country with rivers aplenty, blessed with natural forest and numerous waterfalls.

The Kruger National Park where two million hectares of eastern Lowveld have been reserved exclusively for the protection of Africa's most unique asset – nature's kingdom of animals, birds, insects and plants. The Kruger National Park and adjoining private reserves offering exclusive accommodation, have attracted visitors from every corner of the earth to view The Big Five in their natural habitat, and Africa's wildlife heritage at close range. The Park allows a privileged glimpse of nature in its most pristine and lovely state.

Mopani camp overlooking Pioneer Dam, Kruger National Park

A baobab tree towers over Lowveld grasses and shrubs, Kruger National Park | III

The bustling hub of South African commerce and industry rests across two cities – Pretoria and Johannesburg, and together they form the heart of the Gauteng Province. The profile of dusty, disused mine dumps recalls Johannesburg's days as the City of Gold. A stone bearing traces of gold was found by an unemployed miner in 1886 – and the subsequent discovery of the world's richest natural gold deposits turned this patch of insignificant veld into the international gold capital. The economic boom which ensued established the city of Johannesburg, and it quickly mushroomed into a concrete sprawl which continues today. Johannesburg – known to South Africans as 'Egoli', an adaptation of the Nguni word for gold – remains the cradle of golden opportunities for entrepreneurial ventures. A booming city, where business is conducted in office buildings set in park-like surroundings and, downtown, skyscrapers seem to compete to reach the highest heights. In this commercial headquarters, fortunes are often found and dramatic and consistent expansion has been the result.

Remnants of the settlement created by the Voortrekkers in the 1850s lend a nostalgic air to much of central Pretoria. The city takes on a lilac haze when the Jacaranda trees are in bloom. Elegant landmarks like the Union Buildings and Church Square, parks, sanctuaries and gardens render Pretoria a city that successfully marries a proud past with an optimistic future. The Highveld area enjoys crisp, sunny yet rather cold and dry winters, with summer rainfall and volatile electric storms.

During the months of October and November the streets of Pretoria are covered in a colourful array of lilac hues from the jacaranda blooms

Downtown Johannesburg – a cityscape of high-rise office buildings and apartment blocks | 115

With the migration of workers from rural settlements to the cities across southern Africa, informal communities have been established on undeveloped land in closer proximity to towns and cities. In some areas, makeshift homes are built from corrugated iron sheets, wooden planks or cardboard, while in settlements like Soweto pictured here, housing is modest, yet well planned. Rectifying the issue of housing is a constant priority for the country's leaders.

A colourful sub-culture has sprung up from the streets of the townships – complete with its own township slang, vibrant art and informal industries like the outdoor hairdresser, the pavement fruit-seller, and the corner 'spaza' shop, and a bustling taxi fleet ferries workers to and from their place of work. Regardless of their circumstances, township dwellers display a hopefulness that this Rainbow Nation will evolve to meet their needs, and those of all her people.

The exotic world of the Lost City, a palatial hotel and entertainment destination set amidst thick indigenous forest and elaborate waterways at Sun City in North West Province. The Palace, an extravagant affair of domes and minarets forms the centrepiece of this multi-million rand development.

Vast fields of yellow sunflowers and endless mealie plantations create a colourful patchwork across the enormous central plateau of the Free State. Predominantly farmland, the Free State is however, also endowed with gold mines. This is a different world of quiet villages, wide open spaces and humble farms bearing Afrikaans names, often inspired by the terrain. A massive layer of sandstone, stretching along the Eastern Free State border with Lesotho, has been fashioned by the elements through the ages into unique, flat-topped rock formations. This exquisite landscape of cliffs and rounded hills known as "koppies" (heads) glows with brilliant reds, oranges and golden yellows in the late afternoon sunlight. The Golden Gate Highlands National Park, proclaimed to conserve 4 792 ha of this remarkable land, is a masterpiece of vast grassland and weathered rock, and is the home of many eland, hartebeest and springbok as well as a variety of birds.

Endless sundrenched plains under a big African sky | 121

The area of Cape coast which stretches from the Swartland north-wards to the Namibian border is known as Northern Cape, a land of curious beauty, rich in minerals, studded with diamonds and endowed with copper. Healthy crops of wheat, delicious fruits and fine wines, abundant deposits of iron ore and a bountiful sea harvest are produced by this westerly edge of Africa. From the wheatfields of the Swartland, the road climbs the Olifants River Mountains and into a river valley dense with citrus trees bearing the finest, sweetest oranges.

Further north, the harsh, dry wilderness of Namaqualand leaves the impression of a seemingly endless plain, too arid for anything to grow. Yet each year in spring, after the winter rains, the veld is transformed into a beautiful rainbow-coloured carpet of blossoms. Many hundreds of visitors make the pilgrimage to Namaqualand to enjoy this celebration of spring before the seasons change, bringing dry, hot days and scorching winds once more.

NEIL AUSTEN | Passionate about the outdoors and intrigued by the power of the camera, Neil was driven to investigate a career in photography after completing his education at University. This career has taken him across the vast length and breadth of the country, in all weathers and seasons, in search of the "perfect picture"... the image that best captures the essence of South Africa.

JOHN HONE | The name John Hone is well recognised among those who are passionate about the uKhalamba Drakensberg. John is avidly concerned with the protection and presevation of this World Heritage Site. For more than 30 years John has been recording the landscapes of South Africa's beautiful environment.

PHOTOGRAPHERS | Photography featured is the work of Neil Austen and John Hone | Neil Austen - Cover, I, 2a, 7, 8, wax paper, 11-25, 27-29, 33-45, 51, 52, 56-63, 68, 69, 74, 80, 98-101, 106, 131, 132 and John Hone - pages 2c, 4, 50, 67, 83, 85-97, 103, 104, 108-126, 136 and includes contributions by Illonde van Hoolwerff - pages 30, 47-49, 54, 55, 70 | Nigel Dennis - page 129 | Roger de la Harpe - pages 64, 76-78, 84, 105 | Rod Haestier - page 73 | Marietjie Kumst - page 32 | Carol Polich - page 26 | Brian Preen - page 2b | Jürgen Schadeberg - page 9 | Lanz von Hörsten - page 53, end pages

Graphic designer | Jeannie Mather

Text | Karen Fair

Produced by Art Publishers (Pty) Ltd

Durban, Johannesburg, Cape Town